THE INSPIRED LIFE

BY CHRISTINE HARDY

yellow pear press

ISBN: 978-0-9905370-3-8
Library of Congress Cataloging-in-Publication data available upon request.

Manufactured in China.
Design by Sara Gillingham Studio.
Vintage Sunburst artwork © Ozerina Anna/Shutterstock.
This book has been set in Vectora and The Hand.

10 9 8 7 6 5 4 3 2 1

Yellow Pear Press, LLC.
yellowpearpress.com
Distributed by Publisher's Group West.

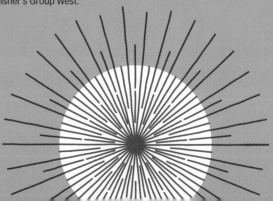

TABLE OF CONTENTS

INTRODUCTION

Growing up with a dysfunctional, drug addicted mother and a caring, nurturing, vegetarian father gave me a front-row seat to both heartbreaking self-destruction and hard-won success. I saw what worked. I saw what didn't. I knew that I didn't want my life to go the way my mother's did, so have subsequently studied how to live a fulfilling, focused life. I've spent a tremendous amount of time and energy sorting it all out and now enjoy sharing what I've learned with others.

There are three *active* ingredients that go into living an inspired life: the *act* of hoping, the *act* of persevering, and then finally, the *act* of becoming triumphant. The key, as you will have noted, is in the *action*. For some, *getting motivated to act* is the hard part, which is why I have compiled these gems of inspiration to mentally and emotionally feed your soul when you feel depleted or are floundering. For others, the hard part might be *an immediate challenge* that fills you with self-doubt: *Am I good enough? What if I fail? Where do I begin?* The quotes, excerpts, and motivational text in *The Inspired Life* will help you find the answers.

Hope and perseverance are the stepping stones to triumph. Hope is the *desire* to change and the understanding that you have to modify your course in order to get where you want to go. Perseverance is the *ability* to raise the bar in your life through action. In this state you are *becoming* whom you need to be in order to be triumphant in an endeavor. In the mode of perseverance, triumph begins to feel attainable. That's where staying inspired comes into play. In order to persevere, you need to stay positive, bold, and proud. You need to take the time to celebrate who you are and who you are becoming.

Becoming a success and living an abundant life are dependent upon your mindset. Triumph requires a purposeful approach, starting with the *hope* that helps you to visualize where you want to go and the *perseverance* to continue the transformation that will get you there. To succeed you have to show up and actively participate *daily*. *The Inspired Life* is filled with helpful advice, ideas, and positive thoughts to keep you on track towards mastery of your goals.

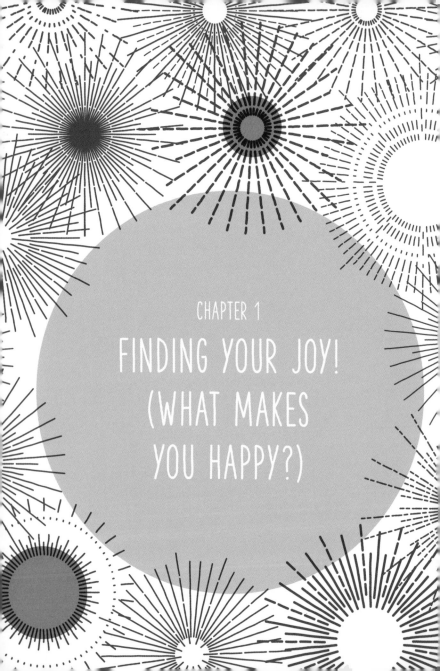

CHAPTER 1

FINDING YOUR JOY!
(WHAT MAKES
YOU HAPPY?)

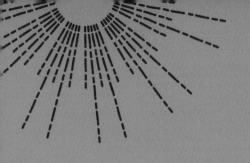

BEFORE YOU GET
OUT OF BED IN
THE MORNING,
THINK ABOUT WHAT
BRINGS YOU JOY.